SPOTLIGHT ON EXPLORERS AND COLONIZATION™

MARCO POLO

Epic Traveler Throughout Asia

SAMUEL WILLARD CROMPTON

Rosen
YA™
New York

Published in 2018 by The Rosen Publishing Group, Inc.
29 East 21st Street, New York, NY 10010

First Edition

Library of Congress Cataloging-in-Publication Data

Name: Crompton, Samuel Willard.

Title: Marco Polo : epic traveler throughout Asia / Samuel Willard Crompton.

Description: New York, NY : Rosen Publishing Group, 2018. | Series: Spotlight on explorers and colonization | Includes bibliographical references and index.

Identifiers: LCCN 2016055907 | ISBN 9781508175032 (pbk. book) | ISBN 9781508175049 (6 pack) | ISBN 9781508175056 (library bound book)

Subjects: LCSH: Polo, Marco, 1254–1323?—Juvenile literature. | Explorers—Italy—Biography—Juvenile literature. | Asia—Description and travel—Juvenile literature.

Classification: LCC G370.P9 C76 2017 | DDC 910.92 [B] —dc23

LC record available at https://lccn.loc.gov/2016055907

Manufactured in the United States of America

CONTENTS

MARCO AT HOME

Marco Polo is one of the greatest of all explorers. Thanks to his journeys, Europeans learned about China and the East, regions that were so far away from them. Thanks to his book, which has been printed many times, the world became better understood.

Born around the year 1254, Marco grew up in the beautiful city of Venice, in northern Italy. There, he walked the stone paths, and rode gondolas around the canals. Marco was happy in all ways except one. He did not know his father.

Niccolò Polo was Marco's father. Maffeo Polo was his uncle. Together, these two

merchants of Venice had departed for the East when Marco was still very young. They reached China in 1266. When the two brothers finally returned to Venice, they had amazing stories to tell.

China! The land of silk and tea! China! Part of the largest empire in the world! China! The land ruled by Kublai Khan!

Marco wanted to see China for himself.

THE QUEST

Niccolò and Maffeo Polo did not remain in Venice very long. After being reunited with their families, the Polo brothers declared they had to return to China. Kublai Khan demanded it.

The wives and children of the Polo family begged Niccolò and Maffeo to stay in Venice, where they would be safe. But the brothers needed to make a living for their families. They were also on a quest. Kublai Khan required them to return with 100 Christian missionaries and holy oil from Jerusalem. The brothers could not refuse this request.

Young Marco spoke up. He wanted to go, too, he said.

Venice was one of the most active merchant cities of the whole Mediterranean world. Marco and his father and uncle left from here in the year 1271.

Now the Polo family really protested. It was bad enough for Niccolò and Maffeo to leave. But to take Marco was terrible. He was too young, they said.

But Marco got his wish. At about seventeen years old, he left with his father and uncle, in the year 1271.

SETTING OUT

The Polos traveled by sea to Acre, in the Middle East. They collected oil at the sacred church in Jerusalem. They only found two priests willing to make the journey to China, however.

Departing from Acre, the Polos and the priests traveled across Turkey and into Iraq. Sun, wind, and heat made the journey difficult. The priests turned back, saying it was too dangerous. The Polos conferred among themselves. Should they also turn back? Absolutely not! They had a commitment to Kublai Khan.

Leaving the priests behind, the Polos traveled across lands few Europeans had

Jerusalem was the center of the world, as far as Christians were concerned. Marco and his father and uncle stopped here on their way to China.

ever seen. They saw humble villages, but also grand castles. Niccolò and Maffeo had been on these roads before, but Marco's eyes were wide with wonder and excitement. He'd soon be crossing high mountains, wide deserts, and fabulous cities—thousands of miles of adventure!

THE MIDDLE EAST

Marco met many people on his journey through the Middle East. He met Turks, Arabs, Persians, Kurds, Greeks, Armenians, Circassians, and Egyptians. The Middle East was one of the great crossroads of the world. Niccolò and Maffeo knew Persian and Mongol, which made the journey easier.

Most of the people Marco met were Muslims, followers of Islam. For 200 years, Christian crusaders had been battling Muslims over control of the Middle East. But the Middle East was a land of many different religions and sects: Sunni Muslims, Shia Muslims, Orthodox Christians, Nestorian

The Crusades made the Middle East a dangerous place, but the new Mongol Empire had brought peace and safety for traveling merchants.

Christians, Jews, Zoroastrians, and mystics of every faith. It may have been a strange land for Marco, but the Middle East was no stranger to merchants from all around the known world.

Marco was fascinated by the different people he met. This quality would be very useful to him when he reached China.

AFGHANS AND MONGOLS

Entering the high mountains of Afghanistan, the three Polos met even more unfamiliar people. The Afghan tribespeople had lived on their own, free from outside influence, for thousands of years. Marco admired them for their ability to live in the high mountains. To Venetians like the Polos, who had been raised near the sea, the biggest difficulty of the area was the lack of water. They were amazed that the Afghans could even survive.

The Polos also met their first Mongols. Half a century earlier, the Mongols had conquered much of Asia. Marco was not impressed with the Mongols he met. They seemed short and rather rude. Later, as he learned of their successes as conquerors and warriors, he came to admire them.

The three Polos were pleased to leave the mountains and to enter onto the plateau of Central Asia. They did not realize that the biggest challenge lay just ahead.

THE GREAT DESERT

More than two years had passed, and the Polos still had not reached China. The closer they came, the more the dangers increased. After long travel, the Polos and their camel drivers came to the edge of a vast desert that today we call the Taklimakan Desert.

They would have to cross with great speed, the drivers said. Otherwise, their supply of water would not last. So the Polos and their companions set out across the great desert. Days and weeks of discomfort followed. The Polos went thirsty many times. At night they were tormented by the sounds of voices, which seemed to command them

Marco and his father and uncle often encountered lonely, desolate scenes such as this one. The deserts of Central Asia still intimidate today's travelers.

to return home. The voices were figments of the imagination, caused by the desert winds. The Polos also experienced mirages, meaning they saw water where there was none. If these trials continued, they would die in the desert.

Perhaps two months after setting out, the Polos reached the other side. They fell to their knees, thanking God for bringing them safely across.

THE SUMMER PALACE

Kublai Khan was lord of the Mongols and leader of their empire. The khan lived in what is now Beijing, the capital of China. During the hot summer months, he moved his court to a summer palace in the countryside. It was here, at Shangdu, that the Polos met the khan.

The beauty and magnificence of the summer palace were hard to describe. Marco was awestruck when he saw the lords and ladies, servants and slaves, and bowmen and falconers of Kublai Khan's court. Nothing in Venice, Rome, or Jerusalem prepared him for what he called Xanadu.

When the Polos arrived in China, they were brought before Kublai Khan, the Great Khan of the Mongol Empire. He received them graciously.

Kublai Khan was pleased to see Niccolò and Maffeo Polo again. He was grateful for the holy oil they brought from Jerusalem. But the khan was displeased in one respect. The Polos brought no Christian priests to him. In order to make him happier, Niccolò and Maffeo introduced Marco to him. They offered him as a servant to the khan.

Kublai Khan liked Marco right away.

MARCO THE MESSENGER

The older Polos went to work. They were merchants, and China had the best trade goods in the entire world. Niccolò and Maffeo did well, trading silk and porcelain, among other things.

Marco worked with his father and uncle for a time. Within a few years, though, he became a special employee of Kublai Khan.

The khan needed someone like Marco. The khan received reports from all parts of the Mongol Empire, sometimes from four thousand miles (6,437 kilometers) away. The khan could not always trust the reports. If he gave a message to a fellow Mongol, that

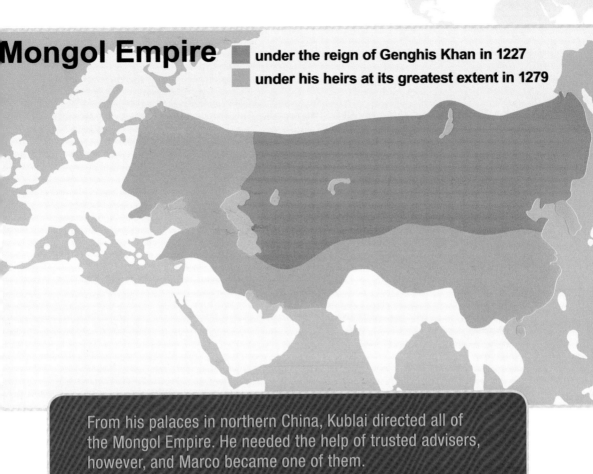

Mongol Empire

under the reign of Genghis Khan in 1227

under his heirs at its greatest extent in 1279

From his palaces in northern China, Kublai directed all of the Mongol Empire. He needed the help of trusted advisers, however, and Marco became one of them.

person might be bribed or influenced. The khan sent Marco to various regions of the Mongol Empire. Marco carried messages to the governors of the different provinces, but he also took notes for himself. He brought back valuable information to the khan.

MARCO THE DIPLOMAT

The longer Marco stayed in Kublai Khan's service, the more the khan trusted him. Marco had excellent eyes and ears. The more he observed, the more he reported. And the more he reported, the more responsibility Kublai Khan entrusted to him. Marco eventually became a diplomat, representing the khan to foreign leaders.

As a diplomat, Marco traveled to Vietnam and Malaysia where he witnessed many unfamiliar customs. His job was to deliver messages from the khan, and to return with messages from foreign rulers. Marco took the opportunity, though, to make notes on all that he saw.

China is where fireworks were first invented. The Mongols of Marco Polo's time loved to have fireworks at their festivals. So do the Chinese of our time.

Whether these notes were made on paper or whether Marco simply used his memory is not known. We do know, however, that China is where paper was first invented and used. Marco was one of the first Europeans to see paper, and also one of the first to observe the explosion of gunpowder, which the Chinese loved to use in fireworks at their festivals.

MARCO THE HISTORIAN

As he traveled through East Asia, Marco learned things no other European knew. Thanks to his closeness with Kublai Khan, Marco knew how the Mongols had conquered their neighbors and built a huge empire. Thanks to his interviews with Chinese, Vietnamese, and Malaysian leaders, Marco knew about the various peoples that lived in East Asia. And thanks to his keen eyes and ears, he knew a great deal about Chinese customs.

Marco became a historian without planning to do so.

A historian listens to stories, collects evidence, and writes about other cultures

As a traveler and historian, Marco Polo came to know large sections of what are now China, Malaysia, and Vietnam.

and times. The role of historian came naturally to Marco because of his many travels. No other person of his time—at least none that we know of—traveled so many miles or met so many different people. The knowledge was in Marco's head, and someday he would put it to good use.

WATCHING GREATNESS IN ACTION

Marco admired Kublai Khan more the longer he remained in the khan's service. Kublai Khan had many titles. He was Lord of the Mongols and Leader of the Mongol Empire. He was Master of Asia. If one took all his titles and put them together, they came out to be something like Master of the Known World.

Marco knew, of course, that there was more to the world than Kublai Khan's corner of it, as large and impressive as that was. He knew that his own European homeland had many good and useful things, though not as grand and beautiful as those of China.

Kublai Khan was the greatest, most powerful leader in the world. But he often listened to Marco Polo, whom he trusted.

Marco did not tell the khan everything about his home for fear that he might wish to conquer Europe. But Marco admired Kublai as a great ruler who did good things for the people he ruled.

Later, when Marco wrote the stories of his travels, he praised the khan so much that some people claimed he exaggerated. Marco never admitted to any exaggerations. In fact, on his deathbed, Marco said, "I did not tell half of what I saw."

LONGING FOR HOME

After years away, Marco was eager to go home. His father and uncle felt this even more strongly. They were older, and they feared they would never see Venice again, if they did not leave rather soon. And so, after fifteen years in China, the three Polos asked Kublai Khan if they could leave.

The khan was angry. He had given the world to the Polos, making them rich. He refused permission and told the Polos not to raise the question again. The Polos resigned themselves to the idea that they would stay in China for the rest of their

By his late thirties, Marco longed for home. He had not seen Venice since the age of seventeen. The longing was natural, but this does not mean Kublai Khan was ready to agree.

BOOK-ILLUSTRATION: FACSIMILES OF ENGRAVINGS.

Woodcut portrait of Marco Polo the Traveller.

From the German translation of his work ; folio, Nuremberg, 1477.

lives. Marco was young enough that he could still have hope, but his father and uncle were ready to give up. And then, just when the matter seemed completely hopeless, the Polos experienced a change in luck, or fortune.

THE MONGOL PRINCESS

Kublai Khan's empire was so vast that he had relatives governing sections of it. One of those relatives governed in Persia, which is now Iran. This relative's wife had died, and he asked the khan to send him a new wife.

The khan selected a seventeen-year-old princess for this duty. She had heard stories of the journey to Persia, though, and feared she would not survive. Hearing this, Kublai Khan had the three Polos brought before him. Would they conduct the Mongol princess safely to Persia? If so, they could go home, he said.

This Chinese noble lady is a good example of the women of Kublai Khan's court. His court was filled with men and women from all over Asia: Mongols, Koreans, Semu, Hui, and Chinese.

Thrilled, the Polos agreed. When the khan declared they could go by sea, rather than land, that made them even happier. The khan did tell the Polos to come back to China after a reasonable stay in Venice, though.

Bowing low, the three Polos agreed to do everything the khan required.

HEADED HOME

Experienced travelers often say that the return journey is the hardest. This may be because the weary traveler has to retrace his or her footsteps. Then, too, the longing for home makes the journey seem longer. So it was with the Polos.

Departing China in the year 1292, the Polos went aboard a fleet of ships. Going by sea should have been easier than by land, but the Polos and the Mongol princess found the journey exhausting. Pirates prowled the southern seas, and the ships had to thread their way through many dangers. Eventually, the ships reached southern Persia, and the Polos safely

Many travelers crossed the Silk Road during the Middle Ages. But few of them came to know that road and the surrounding lands the way Marco did.

delivered the Mongol princess to her new home. Sadly, though, she did not live very long after her arrival.

One last leg of the journey remained. The three Polos crossed Iran, Iraq, and Turkey on their way to the eastern Mediterranean Sea. They then took ships and arrived in Venice in the year 1294.

HOME AT LAST

The Polos were so tired and weather-beaten that even their families did not recognize them at first. But the wealth they brought, the jewels especially, persuaded people that they had indeed gone all the way to China and made it home safely.

Family, friends, and neighbors asked the Polos all sorts of questions about China, and the lands that lay in between. Marco, his father, and his uncle did their best, but they found some things, including the distances involved, difficult to describe. The Polos also had questions of their own. How much had Venice changed, they asked? And what about Italy and the rest of Europe?

Venice was a powerhouse, one of the richest and strongest cities of the Mediterranean. Its wealth increased as a result of the knowledge Marco brought home.

Things had changed a great deal, they learned. The climate had changed, for the colder. The kings and queens of Europe had gathered more power to themselves. One thing that had not changed, however, was the long rivalry between Venice and Genoa. The two city-states continued to argue, and sometimes to fight.

MARCO THE SOLDIER

Venice and Genoa are located on opposite sides of northern Italy. Venice looks out on the Adriatic Sea, while Genoa fronts the Ligurian Sea. The two city-states competed for trade goods. And, in 1298, they went to war.

Marco volunteered as a gentleman soldier. Serving aboard a Venetian galley, or long-oared ship, he took part in the Battle of Curzola. The people of Venice were excellent sailors, but this time they were beaten by the sailors and soldiers of Genoa. Not only was Marco's ship taken, but he was also captured and made a prisoner of war. He was brought to Genoa and put in prison.

Marco fought in the war between Venice and Genoa. Venice is on the northeastern side of Italy, and Genoa is on the northwestern side. Marco was captured in one of the battles between these two sea powers.

Nothing in Marco's previous experience prepared him for this. He was used to being a traveler, a messenger, a diplomat, and a historian. But now he was forced to remain a prisoner of Genoa as long as the war lasted.

Luck, or fortune, came to Marco's rescue again.

While in prison at Genoa, Marco made a number of friends. Like most prisoners of his time, and ours, Marco needed to find a way to pass the time. One thing he found especially fun was telling stories of what he'd seen in China.

Some of Marco's fellow prisoners doubted him, saying he made China seem greater than it was. How could one land, or nation, contain so many people, animals, and magnificent things, they asked. One of the prisoners was so interested that he asked Marco to tell it all to him. His name was Rustichello, and he came from the Italian city of Pisa.

This is the palace that was used as a prison when Marco was a prisoner of war. It was in this building that he dictated his memoirs to Rustichello.

Over the next few months, Marco spoke about everything he had seen and done, and Rustichello wrote it all down. Marco had a terrific memory, and Rustichello was an excellent listener. By this time, Marco had lost hope. He would die in this prison, he said. But thanks to Rustichello, his stories would not be lost.

That was some comfort.

MARCO'S LAST YEARS

Things got better. The war between Venice and Genoa ended, and Marco was released. He returned to Venice, and resumed life as a merchant-trader. His father and uncle were dead, and it was his job to carry on with the family name and business.

Years passed. Marco married and had several daughters. In January 1323, he wrote his will.

First, Marco declared that proper gifts of money, called tithes, should be given to several churches. Then he named his wife, Donata, as his trustee, and left most of his money to her and his three daughters,

Marco was near the end of his long life. He had seen many wonders, and thanks to Rustichello, the world would soon know about China and the lands that lay in between Europe and the Far East.

Fantina, Bellela, and Moreta. And, most interesting of all, he released his servant, "Peter the Tatar" from China, from any obligations to the Polo family. The Tatars were part of the Mongol Empire, and Peter had come all the way back to Venice with Marco.

With all his cares and affairs settled, Marco died in Venice. We do not know the year or date.

MARCO'S LEGACY

Marco Polo is one of the most important explorers in the history of exploration. Though his father and uncle went to China before him, Marco is the one who left a permanent record. The book he dictated while in prison was known as *History of the World* or *Marco Polo's Book*. Thousands, perhaps tens of thousands, of people read it while Marco was still alive. As a result, Europeans learned of China, Vietnam, Malaysia, and most of the lands that lie in between western Europe and East Asia. Marco paved the way—or smoothed the waters—for later explorers like Christopher

This may be the best tribute of all. The statue is of Marco Polo the traveler, the person who crossed all of Asia, and the Middle East, on foot.

Columbus and Ferdinand Magellan. Thanks to Marco, they knew about China and were inspired to reach it by sea.

Fun! Adventure! Danger! Marco Polo's life was filled with all three, and as a result, he left a powerful legacy for the rest of us.

GLOSSARY

city-states Cities that govern territories.

climate Weather experienced over a long period of time.

conduct To carry something out.

diplomat A person who serves the interest of his or her country or nation to the leaders of other countries or nations.

fortune Good luck that people can draw to themselves through their actions.

gondola A special type of boat, propelled by an oarsmen who stands in the back.

historian A person who studies the past.

mirage The false appearance of water shimmering in the distance caused by intense desert heat.

missionary A devoted religious person who attempts to convert others to his or her faith.

porcelain A type of ceramic dinnerware.

return journey Setting out for home after taking a trip.

sect A religious group, often a subgroup of a larger one.

tithe Ten percent of all the money that has passed through the person's hands; usually given as an act of religious devotion.

Xanadu Common English form of Shangdu, the name of Kublai Khan's summer palace. It has also entered the English language as a term that means exotic, wonderful, and a place of rest.

Buffalo Bill Center of the West
720 Sheridan Avenue
Cody, WY 82414
(307) 587-4771
Website: https://centerofthewest.org
The Buffalo Bill Center is considered one of the finest
    places to view and study the history of exploration.

The Geographical Society of Philadelphia
PO Box 67
Haverford, PA 19041
(610) 649-5220
Website: http://www.geographicalsociety.org/
Founded in 1891, the society seeks to promote the
    discovery and appreciation of the many wonders of
    the world's physical and human landscapes.

The Hakluyt Society
c/o Map Library, The British Library
96 Euston Road
London NW 1 2DB
England
44 1428 641 850 (outside UK)
Website: http://www.hakluyt.com
The Hakluyt Society is the oldest and most
    prestigious society that studies exploration.

The National Geographic Society
1145 17th Street NW
Washington, DC 20036
(202) 857-7000
Website: http://www.nationalgeographic.com
The National Geographic Society is dedicated to its
    mission to study the world "and all that is in it."

The Royal Ontario Museum
100 Queens Park
Toronto, ON M5S 2C6
Canada
(416) 586-8000
Website: http://www.rom.on.ca/en#/gallery/recent
The ROM, as it is often called, supports various
    programs related to the history of exploration.

Websites

Because of the changing nature of internet links,
Rosen Publishing has developed an online list of
websites related to the subject of this book. This site
is updated regularly. Please use this link to access
this list:

http://www.rosenlinks.com/SEC/polo

FOR FURTHER READING

Bailey, Gerry. *Marco Polo's Silk Purse.* New York, NY: Crabtree Publishing, 2008.

Burgan, Michael. *Marco Polo and the Silk Road to China.* New York, NY: Compass Point Books, 2002.

Herbert, Janice. *Marco Polo for Kids.* Chicago, IL: Chicago Review Press, 2001.

Holub, Joan. *Who Was Marco Polo?* New York, NY: Penguin Young Readers, 2007.

Morley, Jacqueline, and David Antram. *You Wouldn't Want to Explore with Marco Polo!: A Really Long Trip You'd Rather Not Take.* New York, NY: Scholastic, 2009.

Porterfield, Jason. *Marco Polo: Epic Traveler Throughout Asia.* New York, NY: Rosen Publishing, 2017.

Rogers, Sam. *What's So Great About Marco Polo?: A Biography of Marco Polo Just for Kids.* New York, NY: CreateSpace Publishing, 2014.

Scieszka, Jon. *Marco? Polo!* New York, NY: Perfection Learning Corporation, 2008.

Twist, Clint. *Marco Polo: History's Greatest Adventurer.* Somerville, MA: Candlewick Press, 2011.

BIBLIOGRAPHY

Belliveau, Denis. *In the Footsteps of Marco Polo: A Companion to the Public Television Film.* New York, NY: Rowman and Littlefield, 2008.

Blunt, Wilfred. *The Golden Road to Samarkand.* New York, NY: Penguin Group, 1973.

Frankopan, Peter. *The Silk Roads: A New History of the World.* New York, NY: Knopf Doubleday, 2016.

Hibbert, Christopher. *Venice: The Biography of a City.* New York, NY: W. W. Norton, 1989.

Man, John. *Kublai Khan: From Xanadu to Superpower.* New York, NY: Transworld Publishers, 2007.

"Marco Polo Biography." Bio. Retrieved January 27, 2017. http://www.biography.com/people/marco -polo-9443861

Rossabi, Morris. *Kublai Khan: His Life and Times.* Oakland, CA: University of California Press, 2009.

Rugoff, Milton. *Marco Polo.* New York, NY: New Word City, Inc., 2015.

INDEX

About the Author

Samuel Willard Crompton teaches history at Holyoke Community College in Holyoke, Massachusetts. He has written about a number of explorers for the twenty-four volume *American National Biography*. He has also written books about Ferdinand Magellan and Sir Francis Drake. Crompton has done some traveling himself. He once took a train trip completely around the edges of the United States and from that experience came his *Handy Fifty States Answer Book*.

Photo Credits